LLNL NESHAPs
2007 Annual Report

Nicholas A. Bertoldo
Jennifer M. Larson
Kent R. Wilson

Contributors:

Brent M. Bowen
Gretchen Gallegos
Donald H. MacQueen

U.S. Department of Energy
Radionuclide Air Emission Annual Report
(under Subpart H of 40 CFR Part 61)
Calendar Year 2007

Site Name: Lawrence Livermore National Laboratory

Operations Office Information

Office: U.S. Department of Energy
            Livermore Site Office

Address: 7000 East Avenue, L-293
            Livermore, CA 94550

Contact: Vijay Mishra   Phone: 925-423-8163

Site Information

Operator: Lawrence Livermore National Security, LLC

Address: 7000 East Avenue
            Livermore, CA 94551

Contact: C. Susi Jackson   Phone: 925-423-6577

June 2008

Table of Contents

Lawrence Livermore National Laboratory NESHAPs 2007 Annual Report

This annual report is prepared pursuant to the National Emission Standards for Hazardous Air Pollutants (NESHAPs; Title 40 Code of Federal Regulations [CFR] Part 61, Subpart H). Subpart H governs radionuclide emissions to air from U.S. Department of Energy (DOE) facilities.

SYNOPSIS

NESHAPs limits the emission of radionuclides to the ambient air from DOE facilities to levels resulting in an annual effective dose equivalent (EDE) of 10 mrem (100 µSv) to any member of the public. The EDEs for the Lawrence Livermore National Laboratory (LLNL) site-wide maximally exposed members of the public from operations in 2007 are summarized here.

- Livermore site: 0.0031 mrem (0.031 µSv) (42% from point source emissions, 58% from diffuse source emissions). The point source emissions include gaseous tritium modeled as tritiated water vapor as directed by the U.S. Environmental Protection Agency (EPA) Region IX; the resulting dose is used for compliance purposes.

- Site 300: 0.0035 mrem (0.035 µSv) (90% from point source emissions, 10% from diffuse source emissions).

The EDEs were calculated using the U.S. EPA-approved CAP88-PC air dispersion/dose-assessment model, except for doses for two diffuse sources that were estimated using measured radionuclide concentrations and dose calculations. Specific inputs to CAP88-PC for the modeled sources included site-specific meteorological data and source emissions data, the latter variously based on continuous stack effluent monitoring data, stack flow or other release-rate information, ambient air monitoring data, and facility knowledge.

SECTION I. Site Description

LLNL, a DOE facility operated by Lawrence Livermore National Security, LLC, was established in 1952 to conduct nuclear weapons research and development. The Laboratory serves as a national resource in science, engineering, and technology. LLNL's primary mission focuses on nuclear weapons and national security, including stockpile stewardship. Its mission is dynamic and has been broadened over the years to include areas such as strategic defense, nonproliferation, homeland security, energy, the environment, bioscience and biotechnology, and science and mathematics education. LLNL comprises two sites—the main laboratory site located in Livermore, California (Livermore site), and the Experimental Test Facility (Site 300) located near Tracy, California. **Figure 1** shows the locations of the sites.

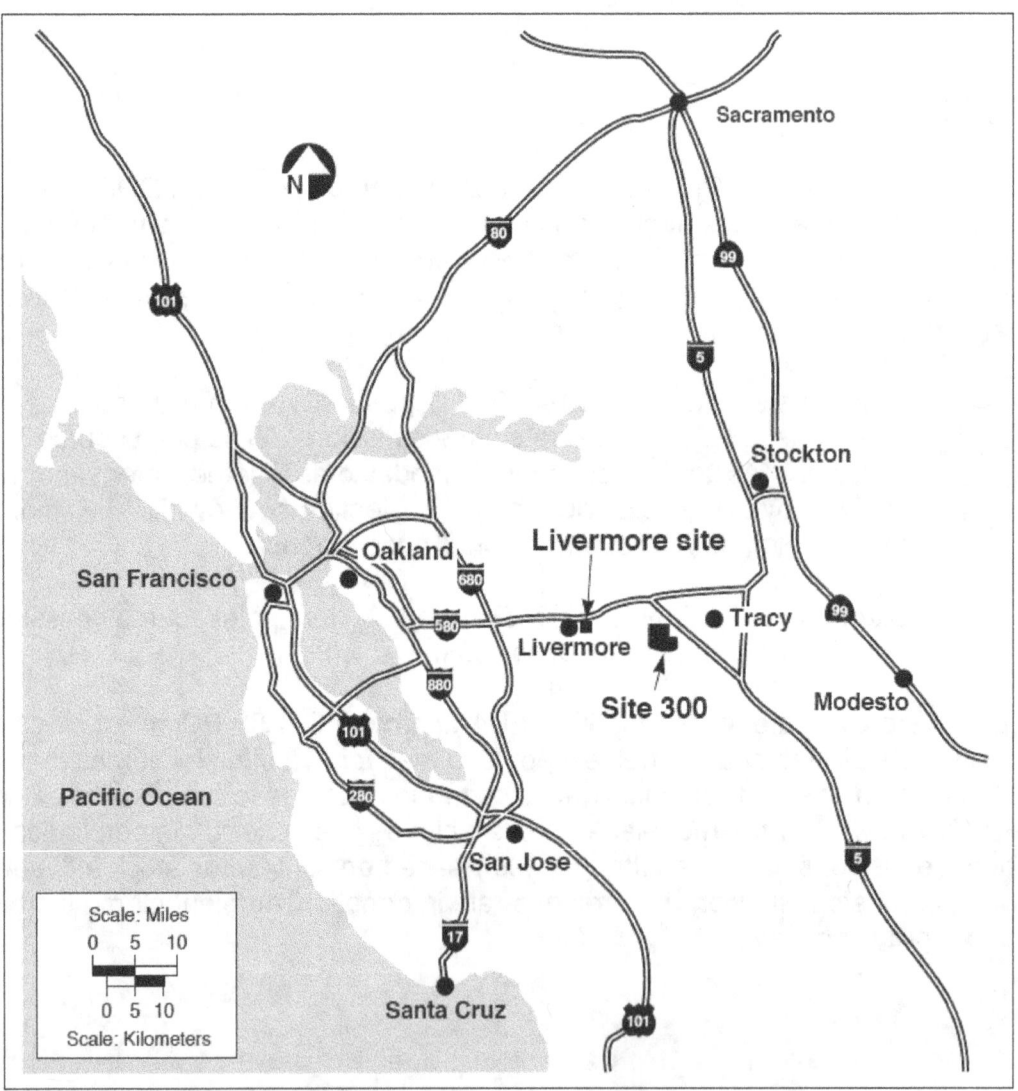

Figure 1. Locations of LLNL's Livermore site and Site 300.

Livermore Site

LLNL's Livermore site occupies an area of 3.3 km^2 located about 60 km east of San Francisco, California, adjacent to the City of Livermore in the eastern part of Alameda County. In round numbers, 7 million people live within 80 km of the Livermore site; about 80,000 of them live in the City of Livermore.

The Livermore site is located in the southeastern portion of the Livermore Valley, a topographic and structural depression oriented east-west within the Diablo Range. The valley is approximately 22.6 km long and generally varies in width between 4 and 11.3 km. The valley floor is at its highest elevation of 220 m above sea level along the eastern margin and gradually dips to 92 m at the southwest corner.

The climate of the Livermore Valley is characterized by mild, rainy winters and warm-to-hot, dry summers. The mean daily maximum, minimum, and average temperatures for the Livermore site in 2007 were 22.6 °C, 7.0 °C, and 14.8 °C, respectively, and the mean hourly temperature was 14.3 °C, typical for the site. Temperatures typically range from –5 °C during some pre-dawn hours in the winter, to 40 °C on a few summer afternoons. The 2007 annual wind data for the Livermore site are displayed as a wind rose in **Figure 2**. In the wind rose, the length of each spoke is proportional to the frequency at which the wind blows from the indicated direction; different line widths of each spoke represent wind speed classes. These data show that winds blew from the south-southwest through west-southwest about 48% of the time and more frequently during the summer (not shown). During the winter, winds from the northeast were more common. The average wind speed in 2007 at the Livermore site was 2.5 m/s (5.6 mph). Eighty percent of the precipitation typically occurs as rain between November and March with very little rainfall during the summer months. In 2007, the Livermore site received 21.7 cm of rain.

Site 300

Site 300, LLNL's Experimental Test Facility, is located 24 km east of the Livermore site in the Altamont Hills of the Diablo Range and occupies an area of 30.3 km^2. SRI International operates a testing site located approximately 1 km south of Site 300. Property immediately to the east of Site 300 is owned by Fireworks America, which packages and stores fireworks at that location. The Carnegie State Vehicular Recreation Area is located south of the western portion of Site 300, and wind-turbine generators line the hills to the northwest. The remainder of the surrounding area is in agricultural use, primarily grazing land for cattle and sheep. The nearest residential area is the city of Tracy (population of over 80,000), located 10 km to the northeast. About 6.2 million people live within 80 km of Site 300. Ninety-five percent live more than 32 km from Site 300 in such distant metropolitan areas as Oakland, San Jose, and Stockton.

The topography of Site 300 is much more irregular than that of the Livermore site; it consists of a series of steep hills and ridges, which are oriented along a generally northwest/southeast trend, separated by intervening ravines. The elevation ranges from approximately 540 m above sea level in the northwestern portion of the site to 150 m above sea level at the southeast corner. The climate at Site 300 is similar to that of the Livermore site, with mild winters and warm-to-hot dry summers. The complex topography of the site significantly influences local wind and temperature patterns. The stronger winds occurring at the higher elevations of Site 300 results in warmer nights and slightly cooler days than at the Livermore site.

The 2007 annual wind data for Site 300 are displayed as a wind rose on the right side of **Figure 2**. Winds from the west-southwest through west occurred 48% of the time during 2007. As is the case at the Livermore site, Site 300 precipitation is highly seasonal, with eighty percent of precipitation occurring between November and March. Site 300 received 18.8 cm of rain during 2007 and had mean daily maximum, minimum, and average temperatures of 21.4 °C, 12.2 °C, and 16.8 °C, respectively, and the mean hourly temperature was 16.6 °C. The average wind speed at the site was 6.4 m/s (14.4 mph).

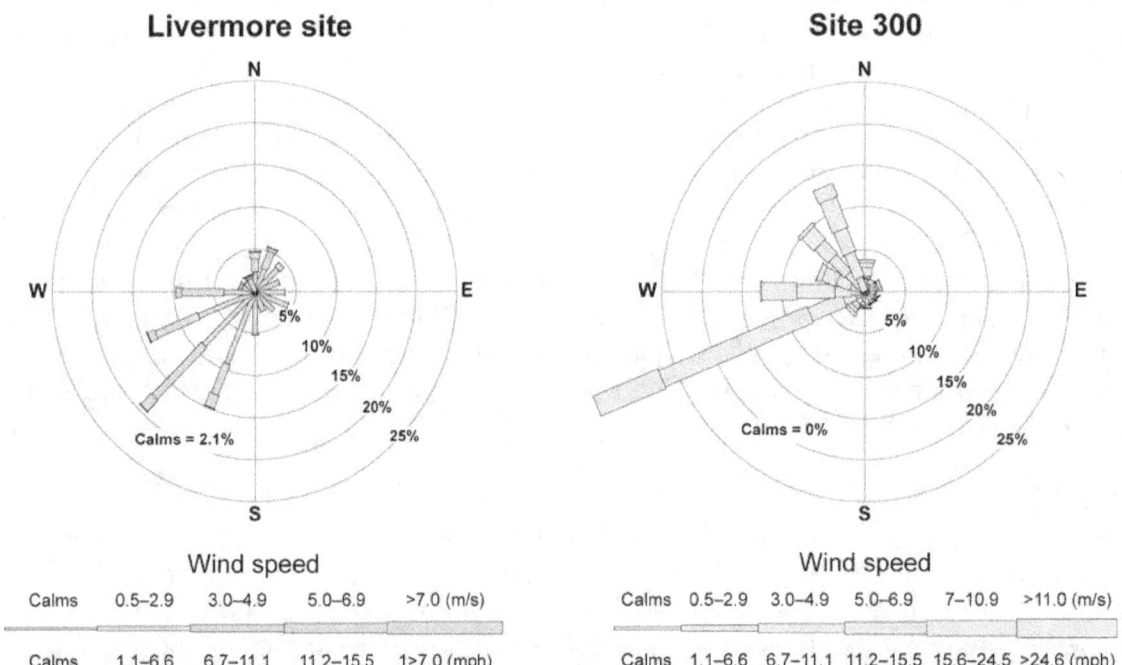

Note: The length of each spoke is proportional to the frequency at which the wind blows from the indicated direction. Different line widths of each spoke represent wind speed classes. The average wind speed in 2007 at the Livermore site was 2.5 m/s (5.6 mph); at Site 300 it was 6.4 m/s (14.4 mph).

Figure 2. Wind roses, showing wind speed, direction, and frequency of occurrence at the Livermore site and Site 300 during 2007.

SECTION II. Air Emission Sources and Data

Sources

Many different radioisotopes were available for use at LLNL in 2007 for research purposes, including biomedical tracers, tritium, mixed fission products, transuranic isotopes, and others—see **Table 1**. Radioisotope handling procedures and work enclosures are determined for each project or activity, depending on the isotopes, the quantities being used, and the types of operations being performed. Work enclosures include gloveboxes, exhaust hoods, and laboratory bench tops. Exhaust paths to the atmosphere include High Efficiency Particulate Air (HEPA) filtered ventilation systems, roof vents and stacks lacking abatement devices, direct open-air dispersal of depleted uranium during explosives testing at Site 300, and releases to ambient air from a variety of diffuse area sources.

Table 1. Radionuclides used at LLNL during 2007.

Hydrogen-3	Nickel-59	Iodine-129	Rhenium-187	Uranium-232	Plutonium-241
Beryllium-10	Cobalt-60	Iodine-131	Iridium-192	Uranium-233	Americium-242m
Carbon-14	Nickel-63	Barium-133	Bismuth-207	Uranium-234	Plutonium-242
Sodium-22	Krypton-85	Cesium-134	Polonium-209	Uranium-235	Americium-243
Aluminum-26	Yttrium-88	Cesium-136	Lead-210	Uranium-236	Curium-244
Phosphorus-32	Strontium-90	Cesium-137	Radium-226	Neptunium-237	Plutonium-244
Chlorine-36	Technetium-99	Cerium-144	Thorium-228	Plutonium-238	Curium-248
Potassium-40	Technetium-99m	Gadolinium-148	Thorium-229	Uranium-238	Californium-249
Manganese-54	Ruthenium-106	Europium-152	Thorium-230	Plutonium-239	
Cobalt-57	Tin-113	Europium-154	Protactinium-231	Plutonium-240	
Cobalt-58	Antimony-125	Europium-155	Thorium-232	Americium-241	

Sources of radioactive material emissions to air at LLNL are divided into two categories for purposes of evaluating NESHAPs compliance: point sources and diffuse area sources. The former includes stacks, roof vents, and explosive experiments conducted on Site 300's firing tables; the latter are, for the most part, dedicated waste accumulation areas and other areas of known contamination, generally external to buildings.

Air Monitoring in 2007

Continuous stack-effluent sampling systems at selected LLNL facilities and ambient air monitors in place at numerous locations on and off LLNL sites are described in this section.

Continuous Stack Air Effluent Monitoring

Actual measurements of radioactivity in air and effluent flow are the basis for reported emissions from continuously monitored sources. In 2007, there were seven buildings (Buildings 235, 251, 331, 332, 491, and 695/696; the last two share a common stack) at the Livermore site and one building (the Contained Firing Facility, Building 801A) at Site 300 that had radionuclide air effluent monitoring systems. These buildings are listed in **Table 2**, along with the number of samplers, the types of samplers, and the analytes of interest.

Table 2. Air effluent sampling systems and locations.

Building	Facility	Analytes	Sample type	Number of samplers
235	Chemistry, Materials, Earth and Life Sciences	Gross α, β on particles	Filter	1
251[a]	Heavy Elements Unhardened[b] area	Gross α, β particles	Filters	23
	Hardened[b] area	Gross α, β on particles	Filters	4
		Gross α, β on particles	CAM[c]	2
331	Tritium	Gaseous tritium/ tritiated water vapor	Ionization Chamber[c]	4
		Gaseous tritium/ tritiated water vapor	Glycol Bubblers	2
332	Plutonium	Gross α, β on particles	Filters	15
		Gross α, β on particles	CAM[c]	12
491	Isotope Separation[d]	Gross α, β on particles	Filter	1
695/696	Decontamination and Waste Treatment	Gross α, β on particles	Filter	1
		Gaseous tritium/ tritiated water vapor	Glycol Bubbler	1
801A	Contained Firing	Gross α, β on particles	Filter	1

Note: "CAM" denotes Eberline continuous air monitors.
[a] Air effluent sampling at the former Heavy Element Facility (Building 251) was discontinued in 2007 after the facility was de-inventoried of all radiological materials. The facility is slated for demolition.
[b] Hardening refers to seismic reinforcement.
[c] Alarmed systems used for facility personnel safety, not for NESHAPs compliance demonstration.
[d] Isotope separation operations are discontinued; area now used for storage of contaminated parts.

Air samples for particulate emissions are extracted downstream of HEPA filters and prior to the discharge point to the atmosphere. Particles are collected on cellulose membrane filters. The sample filters are removed and analyzed for gross alpha and gross beta activity on a weekly or bi-weekly frequency depending on the facility. In all cases, continuous passive filter aerosol collection systems are used. At some facilities, continuous air monitors (CAMs) are also deployed for sampling. CAMs have an alarm capability for the facility in the event of an unplanned release of alpha activity. CAMs are used for facility personnel safety; they are not used for NESHAPs compliance demonstration.

Detection of gross alpha and gross beta activity resulting from particles collected on the air filters is accomplished using gas flow proportional counters. Analysis is delayed for at least four days from the end of sample collection to allow for the decay of naturally occurring short-lived radon daughters. For verification of the operation of the counting system, calibration sources, as well as background samples, are intermixed with the sample filters for analysis. The Radiological Measurements Laboratory (RML) in LLNL's Hazards Control Department (HCD) performs the analyses.

For particles collected on a filter with a result greater than the minimum detectable concentration (MDC) for gross alpha activity, the filter is recounted a second time. If the second result is also above the MDC, the filter is submitted for alpha-spectrometer-based isotopic analysis to determine whether the activity on the filter is a result of naturally occurring radiation or is reportable as a radionuclide emission from facility activities. The Environmental Monitoring Radiological Laboratory (EMRL) in the Chemistry, Materials, Earth and Life Sciences Directorate performs the isotopic analysis.

In 2007, each stack of the Tritium Facility (Building 331) was monitored for tritium release by the use of ion chambers and glycol bubblers. The release of tritium is either in the form of tritiated water vapor (HTO) or gaseous tritium (HT). All of the stack samplers monitor continuously. The ion chamber monitors are set to alarm at designated tritium concentrations for accidental or off-normal releases. Ion chambers are in place for facility personnel safety; they are not used for NESHAPs compliance demonstration.

The Tritium Facility and the Decontamination Waste Treatment Facility (DWTF) use glycol bubblers to sample stack effluent for tritium releases for NESHAPs compliance. The bubblers use a two-stage glycol impinging process. Stack air to be sampled enters the instrument and flows through two impingers in series capturing the HTO present. Next, the sampled air is directed through a palladium catalyst where oxidation of any HT in the sample takes place, converting gaseous tritium to HTO, which is then collected in the final two impingers (also in series). The impingers are analyzed by the RML using liquid scintillation analysis. This type of sampling quantifies the amount of tritium for both species HT and HTO.

The glycol bubbler at the DWTF is in place as a best management practice; that is, it is not required monitoring. The tritium emissions from the facility are not sufficiently high to cause a 0.1 mrem dose (1 µSv) that would trigger the monitoring requirement. Beginning in November 2006, the bubbler at the DWTF malfunctioned and was sent to the manufacturer for repair. The bubbler was returned to service on June 4, 2007. During that time, the treatment of tritiated wastes was minimal; the total tritium radioactivity treated potentially released to the air was only 0.0001 Ci (3.7 MBq), and is not a significant addition to the measured 0.046 Ci (1.7 GBq).

Results of Stack Monitoring for Tritium

Operations in the Tritium Facility (Building 331) in 2007 released a total of 15.4 Ci (0.57 TBq) of tritium. Of this, approximately 11.4 Ci (0.42 TBq) were released as HTO. The remaining tritium released, 4.0 Ci (0.15 TBq), was HT.

This 2007 level of tritium emissions continues to be low in comparison to those typically seen in the 1980's and 1990's, indicative of a reduced level of operations in the Tritium Facility. **Table 3** displays the combined HT and HTO emissions from the Tritium Facility since 1981.

Table 3. Combined HT and HTO emissions from the Tritium Facility, 1981–2007.

Year	Tritium emissions [a] (Ci)	Year	Tritium emissions [a] (Ci)
2007	15	1993	237
2006	18	1992	177
2005	32	1991	964 (148)
2004	17	1990	1281
2003	110	1989	2620 (329)
2002	36	1988	3978
2001	20	1987	2634
2000	40	1986	1128
1999	280	1985	989 (1000)
1998	109	1984	2200 (5000)
1997	299	1983	3024
1996	215	1982	1914
1995	92	1981	2552
1994	137		

[a] Chronic releases from normal operations are distinguished from acute accidental releases by showing the latter in parentheses. Accidental releases were predominately HT gas. Total emissions for the year are the sum of both chronic and accidental releases.

The DWTF released a total of 46 mCi (1.7 GBq) of measured tritium in 2007. Of this, approximately 44 mCi (1.6 GBq) of tritium was released as HTO, and 1.7 mCi (6.3×10^{-2} GBq) was released as HT. The measured tritium emissions from the DWTF remain low, and resulted in a fenceline dose of only 3.5×10^{-5} mrem (3.5×10^{-4} µSv), well below the required monitoring limit of 0.1 mrem (1 µSv).

Results of Stack Monitoring for Gross Alpha and Gross Beta Radiation

The Contained Firing Facility (CFF) at Site 300 had depleted uranium emissions in 2007. A total of 7.7×10^{-9} Ci (2.8×10^{-10} TBq) of uranium-234, 4.2×10^{-10} Ci (1.6×10^{-11} TBq) of uranium-235, and 4.9×10^{-8} Ci (1.8×10^{-9} TBq) of uranium-238 was released in particulate form. The emissions occurred over a period of eight nonconsecutive weeks in 2007 from planned facility activities with depleted uranium.

The remaining facilities monitored for gross alpha and gross beta in 2007 had results that were either below the minimum detectable concentration (MDC), or had isotopic analysis performed on filters with two gross alpha radiation detections that identified naturally occurring background radiation as the source of the detected gross alpha radiation. Results that are below the MDC, or have isotopic results indicating naturally occurring radiation, are assigned a zero emission value and doses reported for these operations are zero. If MDC values were treated as actual detected concentrations, which would be an extremely conservative approach, the total dose attributable to LLNL activities would not be significantly affected because the MDC is extremely low.

Ambient Air Surveillance Monitoring for Radioactive Particles and Gases

Surveillance monitoring of ambient air for tritium and radioactive particles has been in place since the early 1970s. In 2007, LLNL maintained seven continuously operating, high volume air particulate samplers on the Livermore site, eight at Site 300, one in Tracy, and ten in the Livermore Valley. LLNL also maintained eleven continuously operating tritiated water vapor samplers on the Livermore site, seven in the Livermore Valley and one at Site 300; in May 2007, the tritated water vapor samplers placed near diffuse emission sources outside Building 331 and in the Building 612 Yard were relocated near the western perimeter, and a twelfth Livermore site sampler was added near the site's northern perimeter. The samplers are positioned to provide reasonable probability that any significant airborne concentration of particulate or tritiated water vapor effluents resulting from LLNL operations will be detected. Two surveillance air particulate monitors are placed in the Southeast Quadrant of the Livermore site; their results are used to estimate emissions from an associated diffuse source. Both an air particulate monitor and an ambient air tritium sampler are positioned at the location of the hypothetical maximally exposed member of the public (defined in Section III) for the Livermore site. Data from air tritium surveillance monitors can provide a valuable test of predictions based on air dispersion modeling, and all surveillance monitors can help characterize unplanned releases of radioactive material. Detailed data from the surveillance air monitoring network are presented annually in the LLNL Site Annual Environmental Report (SAER), which is available on the Internet at the address http://www.llnl.gov/saer.

Table 4. Mean concentrations of radionuclides of concern at the location of the SW-MEI in 2007 compared to the U.S. EPA's concentration standard.

Location	Nuclide	U.S. EPA's Table 2 concentration standard	Mean measured concentration	Measured concentration as a fraction of the standard	Detection limit
Livermore site SW-MEI	Tritium	1.5×10^{-9} Ci/m^3	9.7×10^{-13} Ci/m^{3*}	6.4×10^{-4}	1×10^{-12} Ci/m^3
Livermore site SW-MEI	Plutonium-239	2.0×10^{-15} Ci/m^3	1.6×10^{-19} Ci/m^{3**}	8.0×10^{-5}	5×10^{-19} Ci/m^3
Site 300 SW-MEI	Uranium-238	8.3×10^{-15} Ci/m^3	9.4×10^{-18} Ci/m^{3***}	1.1×10^{-3}	3×10^{-20} Ci/m^3

* The measured tritium value includes contributions from all minor sources (including the Building 612 Yard and the Building 331 Outside Yard), Tritium Facility, and DWTF; it is not possible to differentiate the contributions of the Tritium Facility and DWTF from those of the minor sources.

** Note that the mean measured concentration for plutonium is less than the detection limit; only 3 of the 15 values comprising the mean were a measured detection. Only values greater than zero are used in the calculation of the mean.

*** The ratio for the mean uranium-238 and uranium-235 concentrations for 2007 is 0.0071, which is only slightly less than 0.00725, the ratio of these isotopes for naturally occurring uranium. This results in approximately 97% of the radioactivity from resuspension being attributable to natural occurring uranium and 3% to depleted uranium.

Compliance Demonstration for Minor Radiological Sources
With the U.S. EPA's Region IX approval, LLNL demonstrates compliance for minor emissions sources (both non-monitored stack and area sources) through the use of ambient air monitoring data. The method entails comparing measured ambient air concentrations at the location of the site-wide maximally exposed individual (SW-MEI), defined in Section III, to concentration limits set by the U.S. EPA in its Table 2 of Appendix E to 40 CFR 61. The radionuclides for which the comparisons are made are tritium and plutonium-239+240 for the Livermore SW-MEI and uranium-238 for the Site 300 SW-MEI. All 2007 tritium monitoring results from the Discovery Center (VIS) and the UNCLE Credit Union (CRED) sampling locations (shown in **Figure 6** in Section VII) were averaged to represent the SW-MEI for the purposes of this minor source comparison. For the 2007 comparison of the mean measured plutonium-239 concentration to the Table 2 standard, only those concentrations that were greater than zero from the VIS and the CRED sampling locations were averaged to represent the SW-MEI. At Site 300, wind-driven resuspension of soil contaminated with depleted uranium is of greatest interest in the minor source category. Because this is a diffuse source covering a wide area, the average of the results for all monitoring locations at the site is used to represent the SW-MEI.

The measured concentrations at the SW-MEI are presented in **Table 4**. Also shown in **Table 4** are the U.S. EPA's standards from Table 2 of Appendix E to 40 CFR 61. As demonstrated by the calculation of the fraction of the standard, LLNL's measured concentrations in air for tritium, plutonium-239+240, and uranium-238 are a fraction 0.002 or less of the standard for these radionuclides.

The LLNL radiological facilities included in the "minor sources" classification in 2007 are listed in **Table 5**. In addition, out-gassing tritiated wastes that are stored in transportainers at various locations on-site are also categorized as minor sources.

Table 5. Buildings with minor radiological emissions (i.e., without stack monitoring) by directorate for 2007.[a]

Dir. Off.	S&T		GS	WCI	NIF & Phot. Sci.	Ops. & Bus.
B253	B131	B322	B132N	B612	B162	B419
B254	B132N	B327		B625	B298	B597
B255	B151	B341		B697	B381	
	B194	B361		B804		
	B231	B362		B850		
	B241	B363				
	B243	B364				
	B281	B378				
	B282	B810A				
	B292	B810B				
	B321					

[a] Abbreviations refer to Director's Office (Dir. Off.), Science and Technology Principal Directorate (S&T), Global Security Principal Directorate (GS), Weapons and Complex Integration Principal Directorate (WCI), National Ignition Facility and Photon Science (NIF & Phot. Sci.) and Operations and Business Principal Directorate (Ops. & Bus.).

Radionuclide Usage Inventories

Radionuclide usage inventories were utilized in 2007 to calculate public dose impacts only for the open-air explosives experiments at Site 300 (see Attachment 1) and for pre-start evaluations for various other radiological activities/experiments that commenced operations in 2007.

Radionuclide usage inventory documentation and pre-start evaluations are archived in the NESHAPs data library maintained by the Terrestrial and Atmospheric Monitoring and Modeling (TAMM) Division in the Environmental Protection Department.

SECTION III. Dose Assessment Methods & Concepts

Description of the Air Dispersion and Dose Model

Most estimates of individual and collective radiological doses to the public from LLNL operations were obtained using the U.S. EPA's computer code, CAP88-PC. The four principal pathways—internal exposures from inhalation of air, ingestion of drinking water (for tritium only) and foodstuff, external exposures through irradiation from contaminated ground, and immersion in contaminated air—are evaluated by CAP88-PC. The doses are expressed as whole-body effective dose equivalents (EDEs), in units of mrem/y (1 mrem = 10 μSv). Separate doses for Livermore site and Site 300 emissions are reported.

Three potential doses are emphasized: 1) The dose to the site-wide maximally exposed individual (SW-MEI), which combines the contributions of all evaluated emission points to dose at a publicly accessible facility for comparison to the 10 mrem/y (100 μSv/y) standard; 2) the maximum dose to any member of the public, in any direction attributed to each unabated emission point on the site to determine the need for continuous monitoring; and 3) the collective dose to populations residing within 80 km of the two LLNL sites, summing the products of individual doses received and number of people receiving them.

Summary of Model Input Parameters
General Model Inputs

Attachment 1 details the key identifiers and input parameters for CAP88-PC model runs. These include building number, stack ID, isotope(s), emission rate in curies per year (1 Ci = 3.7×10^{10} Bq), and stack parameters, including height, diameter, and emission velocity.

Meteorological Data

All model runs used actual 2007 Livermore site and Site 300 meteorological data collected from the meteorological towers for each site. At these towers, wind speed and direction and temperature are sampled every second and are averaged into quarter-hour increments, time tagged, and computer recorded. Stability is estimated in real-time using the Solar Radiation/Delta method as suggested by the U.S. EPA. The wind speed and direction data are converted into a CAP88-PC input wind file using U.S. EPA guidelines.

Surrogate Radionuclides

Even though CAP88-PC contains a library of 265 radionuclides, it does not contain all radionuclides available for use at LLNL. As a consequence, use of surrogate radionuclides to estimate EDEs is sometimes necessary. The selection of a suitable surrogate is based upon several criteria, including metabolically similar behavior and similar modes of decay and decay energies of the radiation type of the isotope of interest. Once a surrogate is selected, the equivalent source term is adjusted by the product of the initial inventory of the isotope of interest and the ratio of the effective dose equivalent of the surrogate to that of the isotope of interest. In some cases, isotopic analyses of mixtures of radionuclides are not available and the radionuclides used are identified as "gross alpha," "gross beta," "gross gamma," or "mixed fission products" (MFP). In these cases, for compliance modeling purposes ^{239}Pu is used as the surrogate for gross alpha, ^{137}Cs for gross gamma, and ^{90}Sr for gross beta and mixed fission products to provide conservative dose estimates. For a list of surrogate radionuclides, see Table 2-1 in the 2003 NESHAPs annual report (Harrach et al. *LLNL NESHAPs 2003 Annual Report*, UCRL-ID-11367-04, June 2004).

Population Inputs

The population distributions centered on the two LLNL sites are based on the LandScan Global Population 2001 Database (Dobson, J. E., E. A. Bright, P. R. Coleman, R.C. Durfee, B. A. Worley. 2000. "LandScan: A Global Population Database for Estimating Populations at Risk," Photogrammetric Engineering & Remote Sensing Vol. 66, No. 7, July 2000, pp. 849-857. Available at http://www.ornl.gov/sci/landscan). The population distributions were developed using the geographic information system software, ArcView©, to construct sectors in each of the 16 wind directions at 10 distances. The population for each sector segment was determined by running code developed in the LandScan project and distributed with the LandScan Database. Key population centers affected by LLNL emissions are the nearby communities of Livermore and Tracy, and the more distant metropolitan areas of Oakland, San Francisco, and San Jose, as well as the San Joaquin Valley communities of Modesto and Stockton. Within the 80 km outer distance specified by DOE, there are 7.1 million residents included for the Livermore site collective dose determination, and 6.2 million for Site 300.

Land Use and Agricultural Inputs

For agricultural parameters in CAP88-PC, LLNL used mean values for California based on data from the California Department of Food and Agriculture (CDFA 2002. California Department of Food and Agriculture Resource Directory 2002. Available: http://www.cdfa.ca.gov/card/pdfs/cdfa_rd02.pdf). The mean values are shown in **Table 6**.

Table 6. CAP88-PC's agricultural parameter values representing LLNL.

Parameter	Value
Beef cattle density (# cows/km^2)	1.9
Milk cattle density (# cows/km^2)	4.0
Land fraction cultivated for vegetable crops	0.046

For individual dose from ingestion, it was assumed that 25% of the vegetables and meat are home-grown, while the remaining 75% of vegetables and meat and 100% of the milk is imported (i.e., free from LLNL-generated radioactivity). For collective dose, the urban default choice in CAP88-PC was used (in which 7.6% of vegetables, 0% of milk, and 0.8% of meat are home-grown, with the balances obtained from the assessment area exposed to the released radioactivity).

Emission Source Terms

The source term for each emission source in the calculations was determined by one of three methods. For continuously monitored stack sources, the sampling data (curies released per unit time) for each radionuclide were used directly. For minor sources such as unmonitored facilities or activities, ambient air monitoring data were used to gauge the maximum dose to the public from their emissions (see the subsection on "Compliance Demonstration for Minor Sources" in Section II). For other minor sources, such as diffuse area sources, or that were new operations in the year covered by the report, potential emissions to air were estimated based on radionuclide usage inventories and facility knowledge, or the combined use of surveillance air monitoring and air dispersion modeling. Generally, model runs for sources characterized by inventory data utilize "time factors" and U.S. EPA-specified physical state factors. Time factors adjust for the fact that a radionuclide may not always be in the same facility all year or may be encapsulated or enclosed for a substantial part of the year.

The EPA-specified factors for potential release to air of materials in different physical states (solid, liquid, powder, or gas) are those stated in 40 CFR Part 61, Appendix D. These factors are 1×10^{-6} for solids; 1×10^{-3} for liquids or powders; and 1.0 for gases or any material heated above 100 °C. However, the U.S. EPA Region IX has granted approval for LLNL to use alternative physical state factors based on actual physical form for elemental uranium, various uranium compounds/alloys, and elemental plutonium. **Table 7** provides the approved temperatures for application of the physical state factor for each of these materials.

Table 7. List of materials exempted from the "treat as a gas above 100 °C" rule and temperatures at which the various physical state factors apply.

Material	Solid physical state factor	Liquid physical state factor	Gas physical state factor	Year approved
Elemental uranium	<1100 °C	Between 1100 °C and 3000 °C	>3000 °C	1996
Uranium/niobium alloy	<1000 °C	Between 1000 °C and 3000 °C	>3000 °C	2001
Uranium oxide	<2000 °C	Between 2000 °C and 2500 °C	>2500 °C	2004
Uranium nitride	<2000 °C	Between 2000 °C and 2500 °C	>2500 °C	2004
Uranium carbide	<2000 °C	Between 2000 °C and 2500 °C	>2500 °C	2004
Elemental plutonium	<600 °C	Between 600 °C and 3000 °C	>3000 °C	2001

In addition to physical state factors, emission control abatement factors (40 CFR 61, Appendix D) were used when applicable. Each HEPA filter stage was given a 0.01 abatement factor. (However, abatement factors were not used to evaluate compliance with the 0.1 mrem [1 µSv] standard that determines the need for continuous monitoring at a facility.)

Site-Wide Maximally Exposed Individual

For LLNL to comply with the NESHAPs regulations, the LLNL site-wide maximally exposed individual (SW-MEI) cannot receive an EDE greater than 10 mrem/y (100 µSv/y). The SW-MEI is defined as the *hypothetical* member of the public at a single residence, school, business, church, or other such facility who receives the greatest LLNL induced EDE from the combination of all evaluated radionuclide source emissions, as determined by modeling.

At the Livermore site, the SW-MEI for 2007 was found, as usual, to be located at the UNCLE Credit Union, about 10 m outside the controlled eastern fence line of the site, but about 10 m within the perimeter of the site property, as shown in **Figure 3**. At Site 300, the 2007 SW-MEI was located, as in the past several years, at the boundary with the Carnegie State Vehicle Recreation Area, managed by the California Department of Parks and Recreation, approximately 3.2 km south-southeast of the firing table at Building 851, as shown in **Figure 4**.

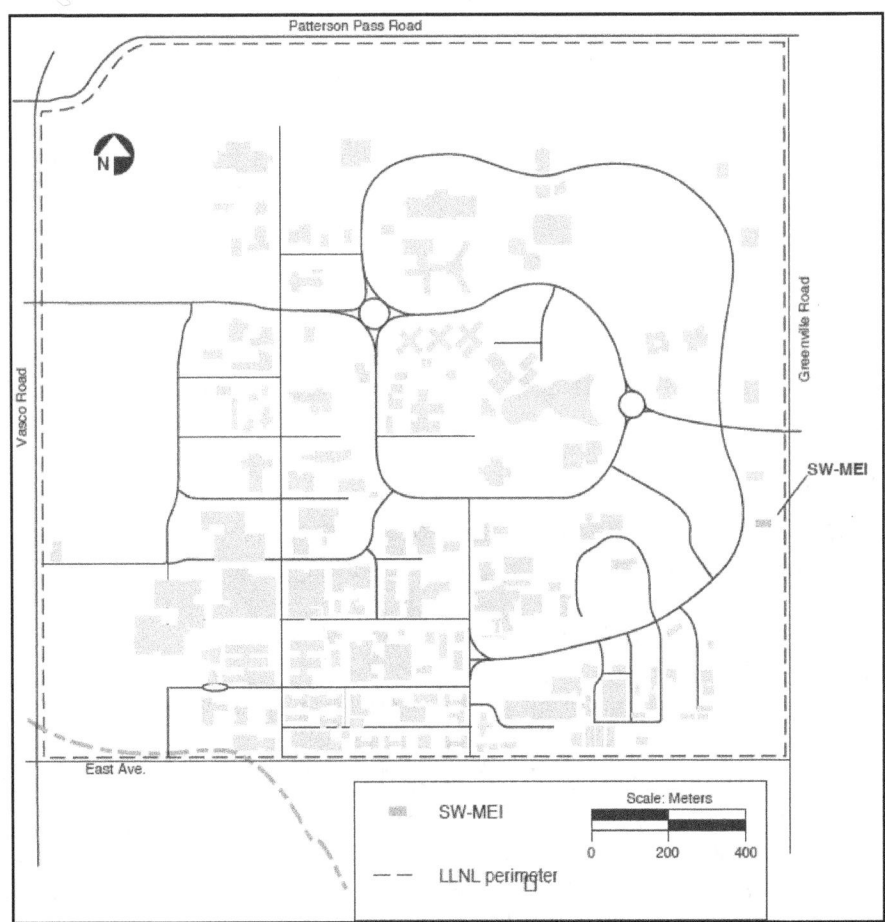

Figure 3. Location of Site-Wide Maximally Exposed Individual (SW-MEI) at the Livermore site, 2007.

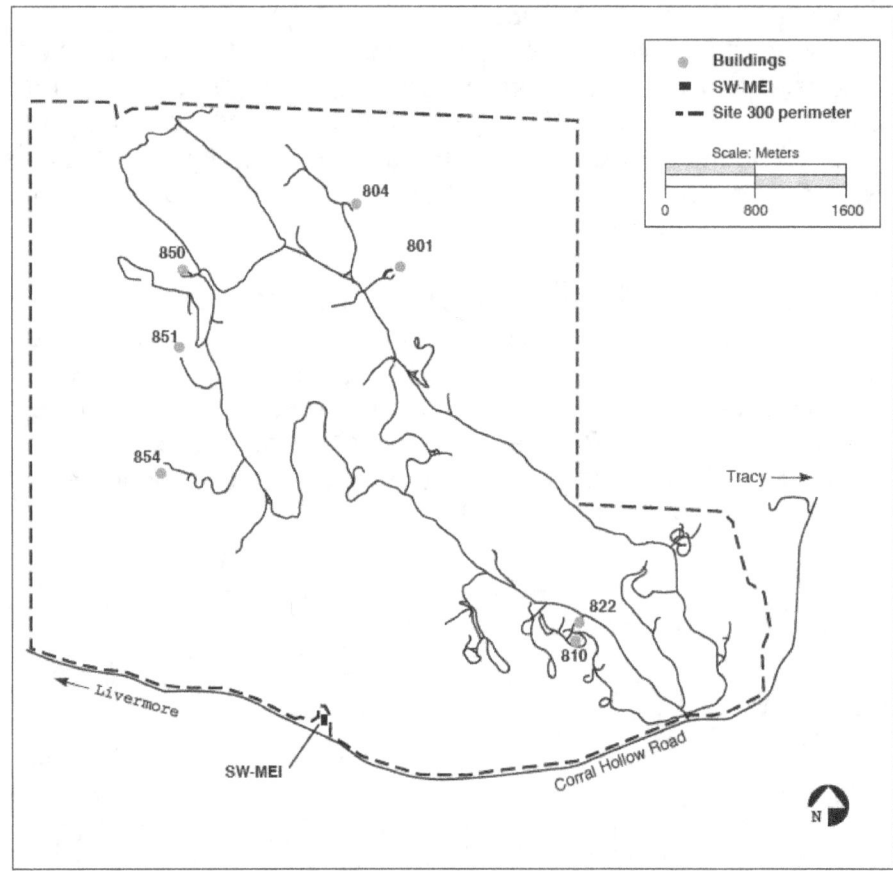

Figure 4. Location of Site-Wide Maximally Exposed Individual (SW-MEI) at Site 300, 2007.

Doses to the SW-MEIs were evaluated for each source and then totaled for site-specific evaluations against the 10 mrem/y (100 µSv) dose standard (see "Total Dose to Site-Wide Maximally Exposed Individuals" in Section IV).

Maximally Exposed Public Individual
To assess compliance with the U.S. EPA requirement for continuous monitoring of a release point (potential dose greater than 0.1 mrem/y [1.0 µSv/y]), emissions must be individually evaluated from each point source to determine the dose to the maximally exposed individual (MEI) member of the public. The location of the MEI is generally different for each emission point, and must occur at a location of unrestricted public access. Typically, this location is a point on the site perimeter, prompting the MEI dose to be referred to as the maximum "fence line" dose. However the off-site maximum dose can occur some distance beyond the perimeter, e.g., when a facility stack is close to the perimeter. Modeling calculations show that ground level concentrations of radionuclides can be expected to reach maximum values beyond the LLNL boundaries for releases from the DWTF stack on the Livermore site. As stipulated by the regulations in 40 CFR Section 61.93 (b)(4)(ii), modeling for evaluation of the need for continuous monitoring must assume unabated emissions (i.e., no credit can be taken for

emission abatement devices, such as filters). Model run documentation typically includes evaluation of the dose to the MEI, specification of emission abatement factors (in place but not credited for the required monitoring evaluation), and the distance and direction to the LLNL fence line point where (or beyond which) the MEI is located; see Attachment 1.

SECTION IV. Results of 2007 Radiological Dose Assessment

This section summarizes the doses to the most exposed public individuals from LLNL operations in 2007, shows the comparison to previous years, and summarizes LLNL's compliance with 40 CFR 61, Subpart H (61.93). Also included in this section are potential doses to the populations residing within 80 km of either the Livermore site or Site 300 and unplanned releases (if any), as requested in supplementary guidance for NESHAPs reporting issued in 1992 by DOE Headquarters, Office of Environment, Safety and Health.

Total Dose to Site-Wide Maximally Exposed Individuals

The total dose to the Livermore site SW-MEI from operations in 2007 was 0.0031 mrem (0.031 µSv). Of this, 0.0013 mrem (0.013 µSv), or 42%, was contributed by point sources, while diffuse emissions accounted for 0.0018 mrem (0.018 µSv), or 58%, of the total. The point source dose includes Tritium Facility HT emissions modeled as HTO, as directed by the U.S. EPA Region IX. (See "Modeling Dose from Tritium" in Section VII for changes [decreases] in the dose from tritium when this assumption is not used.)

This SW-MEI dose is the lowest reported for the Livermore site since 1990, the first year for which NESHAPs compliance doses were calculated. There were no significant changes in LLNL operations or to dose modeling assumptions or methodologies in 2007, and so this dose is comparable to the historically low values reported for the previous two years. The most significant factor leading to this low dose was a continued low level of operations and emissions from the Tritium Facility (see **Table 3** in Section II).

The total dose to the Site 300 SW-MEI from operations in 2007 was 0.0035 mrem (0.035 µSv). Point source emissions from firing table explosives experiments accounted for about 90% of this total, while 10% was contributed by diffuse sources. The point source contributions to dose of 0.0031 mrem (0.031 µSv) is individually the lowest value ever reported and the result is the lowest potential dose ever determined for the Site 300 SW-MEI.

Table 8 shows the facilities or sources that collectively accounted for 99% or more of the doses to the SW-MEI for the Livermore site and Site 300 in 2007. Although LLNL has more than 150 sources with potential for releasing radioactive material to air according to NESHAPs prescriptions, most are very minor. In 2007, nearly the entire radiological dose to the public from LLNL operations came from six sources.

Table 8. Ranked list of facilities or sources whose emissions collectively accounted for nearly 100% of the SW-MEI doses for the Livermore site and Site 300 in 2007.

Facility (Source Category)	CAP88-PC Dose in mrem/y	CAP88-PC Percentage Contribution to Total Dose
Livermore site		
Building 331 stacks (point source)	0.0013	42%
Building 612 Yard (diffuse source)	0.0010	32%
Southeast Quadrant (diffuse source)	0.00040	13%
Building 331 outside (diffuse source)	0.00040	13%
Site 300		
Building 851 Firing Table (point source)	0.0031	90%
Soil resuspension (diffuse source)	0.00035	10%

Table 9 compares 2007 doses with those of previous years. Diffuse source doses were not reported for the Livermore site for 1990 and 1991. In addition, no diffuse emissions were reported at Site 300 for years before 1993, so a comparison of the total Site 300 dose can only be made for 1993 and later.

Table 9. Doses (in mrem) calculated for the Site-Wide Maximally Exposed Individual (SW-MEI) for the Livermore site and Site 300, 1990 to 2007.

Year	Total Dose	Point Source Dose	Diffuse Source Dose
Livermore site			
2007	0.0031[a]	0.0013[a]	0.0018
2006	0.0045[a]	0.0016[a]	0.0029
2005	0.0065[a]	0.0027[a]	0.0038
2004	0.0079[a]	0.0021[a]	0.0058
2003	0.044[a]	0.024[a]	0.020
2002	0.023[a]	0.010[a]	0.013
2001	0.017[a]	0.0057[a]	0.011
2000	0.038[a]	0.017[a]	0.021
1999	0.12[a]	0.094[a]	0.028
1998	0.055[a]	0.031[a]	0.024
1997	0.097	0.078	0.019
1996	0.093	0.048	0.045
1995	0.041	0.019	0.022
1994	0.065	0.042	0.023
1993	0.066	0.040	0.026
1992	0.079	0.069	0.010
1991	0.234	—[b]	—[b]
1990	0.240	—[b]	—[b]

Table 9. Continued

Year	Total Dose	Point Source Dose	Diffuse Source Dose
Site 300			
2007	0.0035	0.0031	0.00035
2006	0.016	0.014	0.0020
2005	0.018	0.0088	0.0094
2004	0.026	0.025	0.00086
2003	0.017	0.017	0.00034
2002	0.021	0.018	0.0033
2001	0.054	0.050	0.0037
2000	0.019	0.015	0.0037
1999	0.035	0.034	0.0012
1998	0.024	0.019	0.005
1997	0.020	0.011	0.0088
1996	0.033	0.033	0.00045
1995	0.023	0.020	0.003
1994	0.081	0.049	0.032
1993	0.037	0.011	0.026
1992	0.021	0.021	—[c]
1991	0.044	0.044	—[c]
1990	0.057	0.057	—[c]

[a] The dose includes HT emissions modeled as HTO. Modeling HT emissions as such results in an overestimation of the dose. This methodology is used for purposes of compliance, as directed by the U.S. EPA Region IX.

[b] Point and diffuse source doses were not reported separately from the total dose for the Livermore site for 1990 and 1991.

[c] No diffuse emissions were evaluated at Site 300 for years before 1993.

Doses from Unplanned Releases

There were no unplanned atmospheric releases of radionuclides at the Livermore Site or Site 300 in 2007.

Population Doses

Population doses, or collective EDEs, for both LLNL sites were calculated out to a distance of 80 km in all directions from the center of each site using CAP88-PC. This air dispersion and dose assessment model evaluates the four principal exposure pathways: ingestion through water (for tritium only) and food consumption, inhalation, air immersion, and irradiation by contaminated ground surface.

The CAP88-PC result for potential collective dose attributed to 2007 Livermore site operations was 0.5 person-rem (0.005 person-Sv); the corresponding collective EDE from Site 300 operations was 0.28 person-rem (0.0028 person-Sv). For the Livermore site, this population dose is attributable to tritium, and for Site 300, the isotopes in depleted uranium (^{238}U, ^{235}U, and ^{234}U). The value for the Livermore site collective dose from tritium was comparable to the dose in 2006, but the collective dose for Site 300 operations was an order of magnitude lower than the previous year, primarily due to reduced operations at the Site 300 Building 851 Firing Table. These potential collective dose values are both quite small and are, in fact, even smaller than any collective dose reported for each of the previous five years. By way of comparison, the collective dose to the roughly 7 million people within 80 km of LLNL's two sites from exposure to the average level of natural background radioactivity in the United States is two million person-rem (twenty thousand person-Sv).

Although collective doses from LLNL are high relative to other DOE facilities, it is because of the large populations lying within 80 km of the Livermore site and Site 300. Even though the collective doses may be the same, a large dose to a small number of people is not equivalent to a small dose to many people. A better way to present the collective doses from LLNL operations is to disaggregate them into categories of individual dose, which demonstrates the tiny doses received by all of the population.

For the Livermore site, population doses from stack and area releases of tritium may be broken down as shown in **Table 10**. It can be seen in the table that the individuals that make up more than 99% of the population received less than 0.001 mrem/y (0.01 µSv/y) and the vast majority received a dose less than 0.0001 mrem/y (0.001 µSv/y).

Table 10. Disaggregations of collective dose for the Livermore site, 2007.

Individual dose mrem/y	Collective dose person-rem/y	Percent total collective dose
0.001 to 0.01	0.0016	<1%
0.0001 to 0.001	0.029	4%
0.00001 to 0.0001	0.47	96%
Total	0.50	100%

Collective doses can be broken down similarly for the shots from the Building 851 Firing Table and the emissions from the Building 801 Contained Firing Facility, as shown in **Table 11**. In this case, individuals that make up more than 98% of the population receive less than 0.001 mrem/y (0.01 µSv/y).

Table 11. Disaggregations of collective dose for Site 300, 2007.

Individual dose mrem/y	Collective dose person-rem/y	Percent total collective dose
0.001 to 0.01	0.0055	2%
0.0001 to 0.001	0.097	35%
0.00001 to 0.0001	0.175	63%
Total	0.28	100%

Compliance with 40 CFR 61, Subpart H (61.93)

Calculations of effective dose equivalents for Livermore site and Site 300 facilities having the potential to release or releasing radioactive material to the atmosphere were found to be well below the 10 mrem (100 µSv) NESHAPs dose standard for dose to the maximally exposed individual members of the public. Tritium accounted for 96% of the

Livermore site calculated dose, while at Site 300, the entire calculated dose was due to the isotopes ^{238}U, ^{235}U, and ^{234}U, in depleted uranium.

In 2007, there were seven buildings (Buildings 235, 251, 331, 332, 491, 695, and 696) at the Livermore site and one (Building 801A, the Contained Firing Facility) at Site 300 that had radionuclide air effluent monitoring systems. (Buildings 695 and 696 in the DWTF complex vent through a common stack.) However, air effluent sampling at the former Heavy Elements Facility (Building 251) was discontinued in 2007 after the facility de-inventoried all radiological materials. The facility is planned for demolition. These buildings are listed, along with the number of samplers, the types of samplers, and the analytes of interest in **Table 2** of Section II.

LLNL remains committed to monitoring stack air effluent from its Tritium Facility (Building 331), Plutonium Facility (Building 332), Decontamination and Waste Treatment Facility (Buildings 695 and 696), Contained Firing Facility (Building 801A), and Chemistry, Materials, Earth and Life Sciences' Building 235. In addition, Building 491 is continuously monitored as a best management practice based on an evaluation of existing contamination and potential for emissions without taking credit for abatement.

SECTION V. Certification

I certify under penalty of law that this document and all attachments were prepared under my direction or supervision in accordance with a system designed to assure that qualified personnel properly gather and evaluate the information submitted. Based on my inquiry of the person or persons who manage the system, or those persons directly responsible for gathering the information, the information submitted is, to the best of my knowledge and belief, true, accurate, and complete. I am aware that there are significant penalties for submitting false information, including the possibility of fine and imprisonment for knowing violations.

Name: Allen G. Macenski
Director
Environment, Safety, Health and Quality Directorate
Lawrence Livermore National Laboratory
7000 East Avenue, L-510
Livermore, CA 94551

Signature: _____ **Date:** _____
Allen G. Macenski

I certify under penalty of law that I have personally examined and am familiar with the information submitted herein, and based on my inquiry of those individuals immediately responsible for obtaining the information, I believe that the submitted information is true, accurate, and complete. I am aware that there are significant penalties for submitting false information, including the possibility of fine and imprisonment. See 18 U.S.C. 1001.

Name: Michael G. Brown
Assistant Manager for Environmental Stewardship
U.S. Department of Energy
National Nuclear Security Administration
Livermore Site Office
7000 East Avenue, L-293
Livermore, CA 94551

Signature: _____ **Date:** _____
Michael G. Brown

SECTION VI. Supplemental Information on NESHAPs Compliance and Quality Assurance/Quality Control Activities

Periodic Confirmatory Measurements

Results of NESHAPs periodic confirmatory measurements (PCM) are intended to support or confirm two objectives: 1) that those operations not continuously monitored do not, in fact, need to be continuously monitored and 2) that radionuclide usage-inventory-based estimates of emissions and their corresponding doses are conservative.

For sources evaluated to have a potential to result in a dose less than the regulatory value of 0.1 mrem/y that requires continuous monitoring under Subpart H, LLNL achieves the PCM objectives by fulfilling the requirements stated in 40 CFR 61.93, paragraph (e) with its ambient air monitoring program. The ambient air monitoring effort includes thirty-two sampling locations with forty-six samplers placed in strategic areas (see the Air Monitoring Programs section in the LLNL Site Annual Environmental Report [http://www.llnl.gov/saer] for a description of LLNL's ambient air radiological monitoring).

NESHAPs Quality Assurance Program

The LLNL NESHAPs quality assurance (QA) program is a multi-organizational effort. Its major components are the LLNL facilities/programs that have continuous stack effluent monitoring systems; the Radiological Measurements Laboratory (RML) and the Hazards Control Analytical Laboratory (HCAL), both in the Hazards Control Department (HCD); and the Environmental Protection Department (EPD). To coordinate the activities of these organizations, NESHAPs Agreement of Roles and Responsibilities (NARRs) documents are in place between EPD and the facilities and/or programs and HCD. NARRs formalize responsibilities and obligations of the organizations regarding many tasks for the air effluent sampling network. Tasks that are addressed in the NARRs include air sampler design and installation, procedures and their implementation, sampling, sample analysis and tracking, maintenance and repair of sampling systems, guidance on regulatory requirements, documentation of the sampling network, reporting, and the archiving of records.

LLNL's QA project plan for NESHAPs is included in the "NESHAPs Compliance Guidance Document and Quality Assurance Project Plan" (G. Gallegos, EMP-NS-S, 2006). This document recites the key elements of the NESHAPs Quality Assurance Project Plan (QAPP) as specifically prescribed by 40 CFR 61, App. B, Method 114. Because LLNL's NESHAPs QA activities are conducted by two LLNL departments, EPD and HCD, the documentation for the elements of a complete quality assurance project plan is independently maintained by these organizations. The LLNL NESHAPs QAPP presents a cross-walk between the requirements of a complete quality assurance project plan, the documents that meet those requirements, and the responsible organizations.

A general overview of these requirements and the responsible organizations is as follows. EPD is responsible for an annual assessment and demonstration of LLNL's compliance with NESHAPs, as documented in the present report. EPD's Terrestrial and Atmospheric Monitoring and Modeling (TAMM) Division is responsible for environmental monitoring; calibration, inspection, and maintenance of all stack sampling activities; air dispersion and dose assessment modeling; assessment (in cooperation with Laboratory Program personnel) of usage of radioactive materials and their potential releases to air in operations throughout the Laboratory; record keeping; and reporting to the U.S. EPA and DOE to demonstrate the Laboratory's compliance with NESHAPs. HCD is responsible for conducting the stack sampling and radiological analyses. HCD is also responsible for assuring the quality of the samples, sample tracking, and analytical quality control. The LLNL Assurance Review Office periodically audits EPD and HCD activities.

Based on the key elements addressed by the LLNL QA program as presented in LLNL's NESHAPs QAPP, LLNL has met the requirements prescribed by 40 CFR 61, App. B. Method 114 to: 1) identify organizational structure, functional responsibilities, levels of authority, and lines of communication; 2) establish administrative controls; 3) describe sample collection and analyses procedures; 4) document objectives of the QA program; 5) establish a quality control program; 6) establish a sample tracking system; 7) perform maintenance, calibration, and field checks; 8) perform audits; 9) establish a corrective action program; 10) prepare periodic reports; and 11) document the QA program.

Evaluation of New Radiological Projects

The TAMM Division is informed by several mechanisms of proposed new operations and modified operations where significant changes in radiological usage inventories occur. These include reviews of National Environmental Policy Act (NEPA) documentation, Integration Work Sheets, Occupational Safety Plans (describing facility-specific safety procedures and plans), and knowledge derived from participation on EPD's Environmental Support Teams (ESTs). In the NESHAPs context, the EST representatives from the TAMM Division and the Environmental Operations Division (EOD) have primary responsibilities. Written communications between NESHAPs analysts and project principal investigators, including records of model runs carried out to evaluate the need for monitoring of radiological releases and the need to obtain permission from the U.S. EPA to start up operations, are retained in the TAMM Division for at least the period of time specified in 40 CFR 61, Subpart H.

Quality Control for 2007 Air Dispersion and Dose Assessment Model Runs

The only radiological facilities or projects providing an accounting by means of radionuclide inventories were ones commencing operation in 2007 or unmonitored point source releases that contributed significantly in 2007 to the dose to the public. The former underwent NESHAPs evaluation in which NEPA or other documents such as Integration Work Sheets and Occupational Safety Plans were examined prior to start-up of operations, and CAP88-PC model runs were performed to determine the maximum potential doses to the public from the activities. The latter were nine explosives experiments conducted in 2007 at Firing Table 851 at Site 300. Both the input data and model runs for all nine explosives experiments were independently checked and validated.

Model runs were performed for about one dozen sources in the 2007 assessment, including the activities mentioned above and three stack-monitored facilities, two that released tritium to air at the Livermore site (the Tritium Facility and Decontamination and Waste Treatment Facility [DWTF]) and one that released depleted uranium to air at Site 300 (the Contained Firing Facility). More than half of all model runs were recalculated independently. Facility personnel reviewed and concurred with source term data inferred by the NESHAPs analysts for the Building 331 Outside Yard. Copies of individual model runs, including input parameters and resultant calculated doses, are archived in the records kept by the TAMM Division.

Based on these quality control efforts, the data, results, and conclusions presented in this report meet applicable quality assurance objectives.

Changes in Meteorological Equipment

A new 52-m (170-ft) meteorological tower was installed at Site 300 in 2007; this new tower and the old 8-m (26-ft) tower in use since 1979 provided simultaneous measurements during 2007 for continuity and to observe any differences between the two tower locations. The old tower was retired in early 2008.

The wind roses for the time that the two towers were active at Site 300 are similar but they do show subtle differences. The data from the old tower indicate a distinct maximum from the west-southwest and less from the west, while the data from the new tower has the peak spread over the southwest and west-southwest sectors. Similarly the old tower data indicates a secondary peak of winds blowing from the northwest and north-northwest while the secondary peak at the new tower includes a slightly greater frequency of winds from adjacent sectors (west-northwest and north). Possible explanations for these subtle differences are that the new tower is located on grassy terrain and just downwind of higher terrain while the old tower is located on a small hill and therefore experiences less frictional effect from the ground. The new tower is also located at a slightly higher elevation and possibly receives more mixing from higher winds. Wind files from the old tower were used for 2007 CAP88-PC model runs.

U.S. EPA Site Visit

On September 4, 2007, two U.S. EPA officials, Shelly Rosenblum (U.S. EPA, Region IX) and Behram Shroff (U.S. EPA Headquarters), visited LLNL to tour representative facilities and discuss compliance issues. The U.S. EPA officials were taken to the DWTF facility to see how stack monitoring operations are conducted. They were given briefings on the ambient monitoring systems for air particulate and air tritium that are used to demonstrate compliance for minor sources of emissions, and on the real-time monitoring networks. Also discussed were the meteorological tower upgrades, the tritium dose reconstruction of historical LLNL tritium releases and the radionuclide NESHAPs reporting requirements.

SECTION VII. Supplementary Information on Radiological Dose Assessment for 2007

Livermore Site Principal Diffuse Sources

The dose evaluations for diffuse sources at the Livermore site in 2007 required two different modeling approaches. The Building 331 Outside Yard and the Building 612 Yard emissions estimates were based on calculations: unit source terms in model runs for both sources were adjusted simultaneously to achieve a best fit between the CAP88-PC air concentrations from these sources and the B331 stacks (known source term) combined and the air surveillance monitoring data (see discussion of Comparison of 2007 Modeling Results with Tritium Surveillance Air Monitoring Data below). After the source term was determined, the dose from each of these diffuse sources was calculated using CAP88-PC. Air surveillance monitoring data for plutonium from two ambient air monitors at the location of the SW-MEI and at the Discovery Center were used directly to evaluate the dose from historical plutonium contamination in the Southeast Quadrant.

Building 331 Outside Yard

As the Tritium Facility (Building 331) conducts operations, tritium-contaminated equipment and material slated for disposal are packaged in a storage area, removed from the building to outside storage containers, and finally sent to Radioactive and Hazardous Waste Management Division (RHWM) facilities. During 2007, outgassing from such waste released an estimated 1.4 Ci (5.1×10^{10} Bq) of tritium to the atmosphere outside Building 331. This amount was derived from a combination of environmental surveillance monitoring data and tritium facility emissions, and agreed with estimates based on process and facility knowledge. Its release was modeled in CAP88-PC leading to a calculated 2007 dose to the SW-MEI of 4.0×10^{-4} mrem (4.0×10^{-3} µSv).

Building 612 Yard

The Building 612 Yard is a potential source of diffuse emissions of tritium. This area is dedicated to hazardous waste, radioactive waste, and mixed waste management activities. The yard consists of several areas where waste containers are stacked outdoors. Several of these containers outgas tritium. A diffuse source emission of 0.55 Ci/y (2.0×10^{10} Bq/y) from the Building 612 Yard combined with emissions from the B331 Outside Yard and B331 stacks was required to produce the concentrations measured at the Livermore site air samplers. This source term produced a CAP88-PC calculated 2007 dose to the SW-MEI from the Building 612 Yard of 1.0×10^{-3} mrem (1.0×10^{-2} µSv).

Southeast Quadrant

The Southeast Quadrant of the Livermore site has plutonium in the surface soil (from historic waste management operations) and air (from resuspension). A high volume air particulate sampler is located adjacent to the UNCLE Credit Union (the location of the SW-MEI) and a second sampler is located next to the Discovery Center to monitor the plutonium levels in this area. Monitoring data from these air samplers were used as a direct measurement of potential dose via the air pathway. The 2007 mean annual concentration in air of $^{239+240}$Pu (alpha spectroscopy does not distinguish between ^{239}Pu and ^{240}Pu) for all results greater than zero was 1.6×10^{-19} Ci/m^3 (5.9×10^{-9} Bq/m^3). Using the dose conversion factor of 3.08×10^5 mrem/µCi (8.32×10^{-5} Sv/Bq) from Federal Guidance Report No. 11, EPA-520/1-88-020, U.S. Environmental Protection Agency (1988) for ^{239}Pu and ^{240}Pu, and the reference man breathing rate of 8400 m^3/y (International Commission on Radiological Protection [ICRP], 1975, *Reference Man: Anatomical Physiological and Metabolic Characteristics*. Oxford: Pergamon Press; ICRP Publication 23), the dose was determined to be 4.0×10^{-4} mrem (4.0×10^{-3} µSv) for 2007.

Site 300 Principal Diffuse Sources

Diffuse sources at Site 300 predominantly feature the radioisotopes in depleted uranium, with trace amounts of tritium being the only other radiological component of concern as having potential for release to air.

Tritium Evaporation and Migration at Site 300

Tritium gas and solids containing tritium (Li^{3}H) were components of explosives assemblies tested on the firing tables during experiments in years past. Most of the gaseous tritium escaped to the atmosphere during the tests, but some of the solid Li^{3}H remained as residue in the firing table gravel. Rainwater and dust-control rinse water percolated through the gravel, causing the tritium to migrate into the subsurface soil and, in some cases, eventually to the ground water. Tritium contaminated gravel was removed from the firing tables in 1988 and disposed in the Pit 7 landfill. Tritium in landfills, firing table soils, and ground water are potential sources of diffuse emissions of tritium to the atmosphere at Site 300. LLNL personnel maintain an air tritium sampler at a perimeter location at Site 300, and doses from diffuse tritium sources may be estimated based on the monitoring data for that sampling location. For the calendar year 2007, all results in ambient air at the Site 300 perimeter location were at or near the minimum detection limit of the analytical method (about 0.67 pCi [25 mBq]/m^3).

Resuspension of Depleted Uranium in Soil at Site 300

Depleted uranium is currently used and has been used as a component of explosives test assemblies over many years. It remains as a residue in surface soils, especially near the firing tables. Because surface soil is subject to resuspension by the action of wind, rain, and other environmental disturbances, the collective effects of surface soil uranium residuals on off-site doses were evaluated.

The contribution to measured uranium activities arising from naturally occurring uranium (NU) can be distinguished from depleted uranium (DU) contributed by LLNL operations. (A derivation of the arithmetic calculation used for this purpose was presented in Gallegos et al., *LLNL NESHAPs 1995 Annual Report*, UCRL-ID-113867-96, June 1996.) We base our dose estimate for resuspended DU on the measured environmental surveillance monitoring total concentration in air of uranium-238, subtracting out the part contributed by NU, from the following equation:

$$\mu = \frac{0.00726 - 0.99274 \dfrac{M(CU-235)}{M(CU-238)}}{0.00526 \dfrac{M(CU-235)}{M(CU-238)} + 0.00526}$$

where µ is the fraction (by weight) of uranium contributed by operations, CU is composite uranium (both DU and NU), M(CU-235) is the mass of U-235 in the composite (measured) uranium, and M(CU-238) is the mass of U-238 in the composite (measured) uranium.

For 2007, all eight air-particulate monitors at Site 300 were used to determine the annual-average concentrations of isotopes U-238 and U-235. These site-average values gave an estimate of 3.5×10^{-4} mrem (3.5×10^{-3} µSv) for the SW-MEI dose resulting from resuspension of DU in soil for 2007. (For more information on the sampling data, see the "Air Monitoring Programs" chapter in LLNL's Site Annual Environmental Report for 2007, available at http://www.llnl.gov/saer.)

Modeling Dose from Tritium

To evaluate dose from tritium releases to air, we use the U.S. EPA-sanctioned CAP88-PC code. Its tritium model calculates dose from inhalation, skin absorption, and ingestion of tritium only in its tritiated water vapor form (HTO). Doses from releases of tritiated gas (HT) or ingestion of organically bound tritium (OBT) are not calculated. CAP88-PC's tritium model is based on specific activity and assumes that the tritium-to-hydrogen ratio in body water is the same as in air moisture. Because the specific activity model is linked in CAP88-PC with relatively high dose coefficients for HTO, the model's dose predictions generally err on the high side.

Inhalation doses from unit concentration of HT in air are a factor of 15,000 times lower than those from inhalation and skin absorption of unit concentration of HTO in air (ICRP, 1995, *Age dependent doses to members of the public from intake of radionuclides, Part 4, Inhalation Dose Coefficients.* Oxford: Pergamon Press; ICRP Publication 71; Ann. ICRP 25[3&4]). A release of HT cannot be ignored, however, because HT that reaches the ground is rapidly and efficiently converted to HTO by microorganisms in soil (McFarlane, Rogers, and Bradley, Environmental Science and Technology 12: 590-593,1978; Brown, Ogram, and Spencer, Health Physics 58:171-181, 1990) and to a lesser extent in vegetation (Sweet and Murphy, Environmental Science and Technology, 18:358-361, 1984).

OBT is formed by plants during photosynthesis and is incorporated by animals when ingested. Animals also metabolize some OBT from ingested or inhaled HTO. The ICRP dose coefficient for OBT is about 2.3 times higher than that of HTO because the biological half-life of OBT in the body is longer than that of HTO, which is eliminated at the same rate as body water. Although doses predicted by CAP88-PC are generally high enough to account for dose from ingested OBT, a model that explicitly calculates dose from OBT is preferable.

A simple tritium model, NEWTRIT (Peterson, S-R. and P.A. Davis, Health Physics 82(2): 213-225, 2002), calculates ingestion dose from both HTO and OBT and accounts for conversion of HT to HTO in the environment following releases of HT. A discussion of the NEWTRIT model was presented in Attachment 2 of the 2000 NESHAPs annual report (Gallegos et al., *LLNL NESHAPs 2000 Annual Report*, UCRL-ID-113867-01, June 2001). At the U.S. EPA's request, NEWTRIT was coded into GENII-NESHAPS, a radiological dispersion computer code (B.A. Napier, et al., GENII - The Hanford Environmental Radiation Dosimetry Software System. Richland, WA: Pacific Northwest Laboratory, PNL-6584 Vol. UC-60, 1988 and B.A. Napier et al. GENII Version 2.0 Software Design Document. Prepared for the U.S. EPA, November 2002). In August 2007, the U.S. EPA withdrew its proposed amendment to 40 CFR Part 61, Subparts H and I to include GENII-NESHAPS as an approved compliance model. However, GENII-NESHAPS, which has undergone a Science Advisory Board review, is available on the U.S. EPA's website at http://www.epa.gov/radiation/assessment/genii.html.

Tritium doses from 2007 Livermore site operations were calculated using NEWTRIT and compared to those obtained by our standard procedure using CAP88-PC (the latter are presented in Section IV). NEWTRIT does not model dispersion, so tritium concentrations in air calculated by CAP88-PC are used as input. For the principal comparison of the total tritium contribution to the Livermore site SW-MEI dose in 2007, calculated using NEWTRIT instead of CAP88-PC, the result was 0.0020 mrem (0.020 µSv), about 21% lower than the CAP88-PC value of 0.0025 mrem (0.025 µSv).

Comparison of 2007 Modeling Results with Tritium Surveillance Air Monitoring Data

A comparison was made between CAP88-PC-predicted concentrations of tritium in air and ambient air monitoring data for nine tritiated water vapor samplers on the Livermore site (designated CAFE, COW, CRED, DWTF, MESQ, MET, POOL, SALV, and VIS). **Figure 5** shows the locations of the tritium air surveillance monitors on the Livermore site. Modeled predictions have been compared with tritium monitoring data since 1997. For the 2007 modeling and monitoring results, the methodology for the comparison was modified from prior years to accommodate the relocation of two air surveillance monitors in May 2007. The two monitors, designated B624 and B331, which had been placed in the Building 612 Yard and the Building 331 Outside Yard for diffuse monitoring, were removed mid-year; two near-perimeter locations were established, called ARAC and SECO (see **Figure 5**). This change affords LLNL more extensive perimeter coverage while simultaneously obviating difficulties inherent in determining accurate source terms for area sources comprised of transitory tritiated waste.

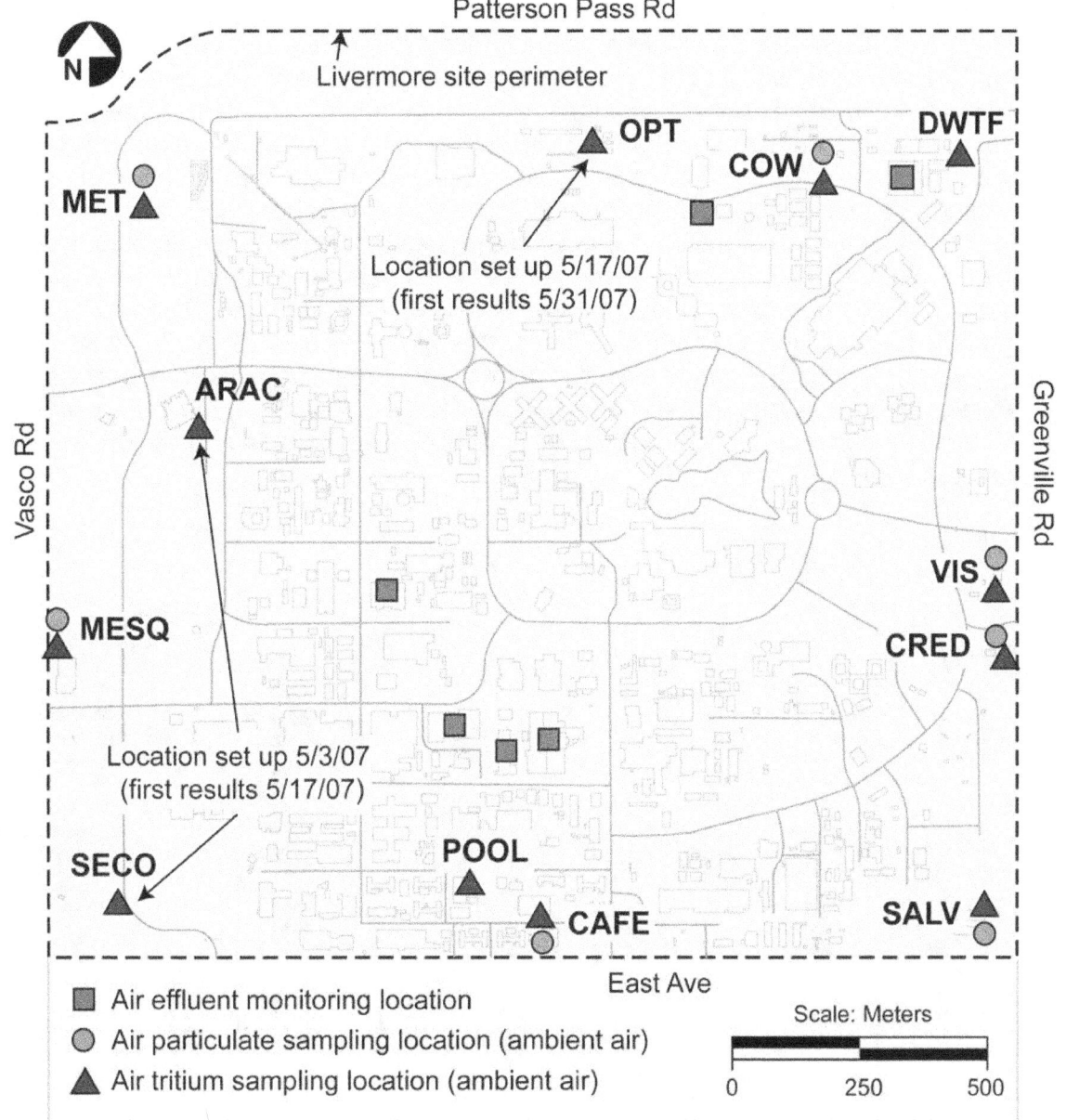

Figure 5. Radiological air monitoring at the Livermore site showing locations for air surveillance monitoring of tritiated water vapor (triangles) and radioactive particles (circles) and stack air effluent monitoring (indicated by darkened squares).

Because the ambient air tritium surveillance monitors only absorb HTO, only releases of HTO from stack and area sources were modeled. Although stack monitoring of the DWTF determined a release of 44 mCi (1.6 x 10⁻³ TBq) of HTO, this release was too minor to influence the overall model-data comparison and so was not included in the model. The release rate of HTO from the two 30-m-high, continuously monitored stacks at the Tritium Facility (Building 331) was determined from stack monitoring data to be 11.4 Ci (4.2 x 10¹¹ Bq) in 2007.

The 2007 tritium monitoring and modeling comparison was conducted based on a "best fit" analysis. Because the measured ambient concentrations include effects from the Building 331 stacks as well as the diffuse sources and because the uncertainty associated with the stack monitoring is much less than the uncertainty associated with ambient monitoring, the source term from the Building 331 stacks was held constant in the best fit analysis while the diffuse source terms were varied to best fit the data. In this method, the distances to the monitoring locations were defined, and distances sufficient to exceed each sampler location were modeled. Unit source model runs were made for each of the diffuse sources; the contributions of the diffuse sources were varied using the open source code language "R" (R Development Core Team, 2008, R Foundations for Statistical Computing, Vienna, Austria, ISBN 3-900051-07-0, URL http://www.R-project.org) until the lowest root mean square value difference between the modeled and measured values was obtained. The results, displayed in **Figure 6**, show that all air concentrations predicted by CAP88-PC were within a factor of three of the measured values.

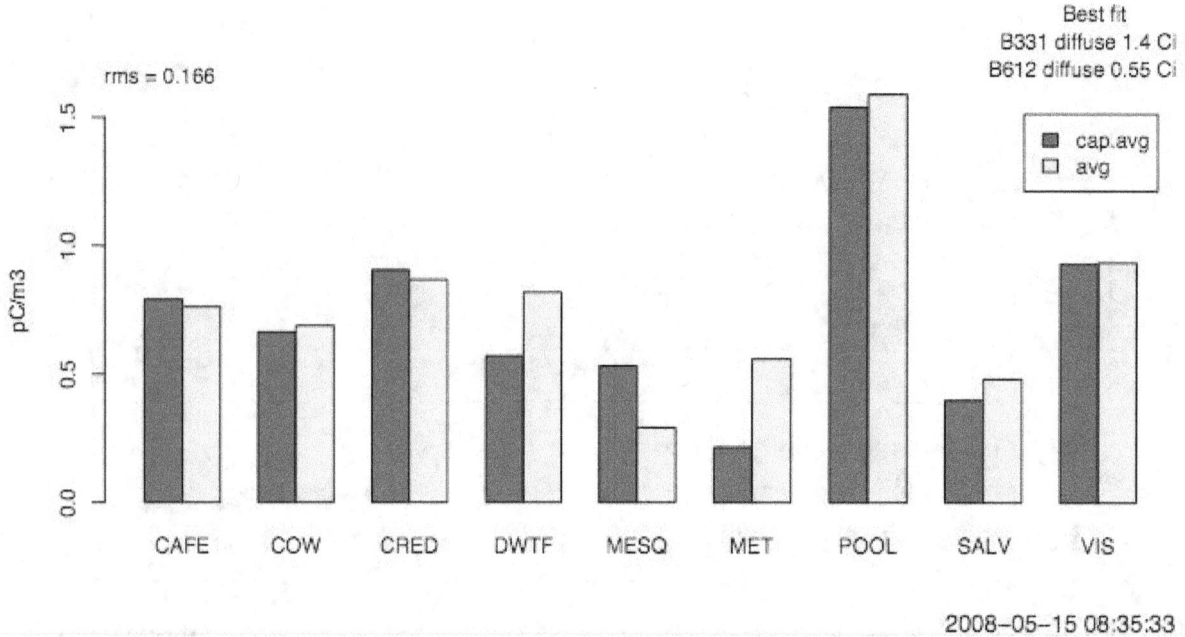

Figure 6. Comparison of measured (avg) and modeled (cap.avg) annual mean concentrations of tritiated water vapor (HTO) in air at Livermore site locations, 2007.

SECTION VIII. Supplemental Information on Other Compliance

Status of Compliance with Other Regulations

Status of compliance with 40 CFR 61, Subpart Q – National Emission Standards for Radon Emissions from Department of Energy Facilities

LLNL does not have storage and disposal facilities for radium containing materials that would be a significant source of radon. Emissions of radon from LLNL research experiments did not occur in 2007.

Status of compliance with 40 CFR 61, Subpart T – National Emission Standards for Radon Emissions from the Disposal of Uranium Mill Tailings

LLNL does not have or store any uranium mill tailings.

ATTACHMENT 1. LLNL NESHAPs 2007 Annual Report Guidance and Spreadsheet

Guidance for Interpreting the Data Spreadsheet
A generalized description of each facility and its operations is provided on the spreadsheet. In addition, the following information is shown for each listed emission point or stack:

- Building and room number(s)
- Specific stack identification code(s)
- Generalized description of operations in the room(s) or area(s)
- Radionuclides utilized in the operation
- Annual radionuclide usage inventory with potential for release (by isotope, in curies)
- Physical state factors (by isotope)
- Stack parameters
- Emission control devices and emission control device abatement factors
- Estimated or measured annual emissions (by isotope)
- Distance and direction to the site-wide maximally exposed individual (SW-MEI)
- Calculated effective dose equivalent (EDE) to the SW-MEI
- Distance and direction to the maximally exposed individual (MEI) for that specific source
- Calculated EDE to the MEI (source term not adjusted for emission controls)
- Source category

Radionuclides
The radionuclides shown in the spreadsheet are those from specific emission points where air emissions were possible. If radionuclides were present, but encapsulated or sealed for the entire year, radionuclides, annual usage inventories, and emissions are not listed.

Radionuclide Usage Inventories
The annual radionuclide usage inventories for point source locations are based on data from facility experimenters and managers. For Building 332, classification issues regarding transuranic radionuclide usage inventories make use of the usage inventory/modeling approach impractical. However, all such affected emission points in these buildings are continuously monitored and emissions are therefore directly determined.

Physical State Factors
The physical state factors listed are U.S. EPA potential release fractions from 40 CFR 61, Appendix D, whereby emissions are estimated from radionuclide usage inventories depending on their physical states for use in dispersion/dose assessment modeling. A physical state factor of 1.0×10^{-6} is used for solids, 1.0×10^{-3} is used for liquids and

powders, and 1.0 is used for unconfined gases and substances heated above 100 °C. Regarding the latter, the U.S. EPA has granted LLNL approved alternative emissions factors for selected radionuclides (see **Table 7** in Section III). These factors are allowed provided that the material is not intentionally dispersed to the environment and that the processes do not alter the chemical form of the material.

Stack Parameters
Stack physical parameters for sources are updated, as necessary, by experimenters and managers for those facilities. The TAMM Division annually measures the stack velocity and sampler flow and calibrates mass flow sensors for each monitored stack.

Emission Control Devices
High Efficiency Particulate Air (HEPA) filters are used in many LLNL facilities to control particulate emissions. For some discharge points, scrubbers and electrostatic precipitators aid the control of emissions. The operational performance of all HEPA filtration systems is routinely tested. The required efficiency of a single stage HEPA filter is 99.97%. Double staged filter systems are in place on some discharge points. Triple stage HEPA filters are used on glove box ventilation systems in the Building 332 Plutonium Facility.

Control Device Abatement Factors
Similar to physical state factors, control device abatement factors from Table 1 in 40 CFR 61, Appendix D are those associated with the listed emission control devices and are used to better estimate actual emissions for use in dispersion and dose models. By regulation, each HEPA filter stage is given a 0.01 factor (even though the required test efficiency that all LLNL HEPA filters must maintain would yield a factor of 0.0003).

Estimated Annual Emissions
For unmonitored and non-continuously monitored sources, estimated annual emissions for each radionuclide are based, as appropriate, on 1) usage inventory data, 2) time factors (discussed in "Emission Source Terms" in Section III), 3) U.S. EPA potential release fractions (physical state factors), and 4) applicable emission control device abatement factors.

Actual emission measurements are the basis for reported emissions from continuously monitored facilities. LLNL facilities that had continuous monitoring systems in 2007 were Buildings 235, 251, 331, 332, 491, and 695/696 at the Livermore site, and Building 801A (the Contained Firing Facility) at Site 300, as noted earlier in the subsection on "Compliance with 40 CFR 61, Subpart H (61.93)" in Section IV. See also the discussion below under "0.1 mrem/y Monitoring Requirement" regarding the use of emissions measurements for monitored sources.

10 mrem/y Site-Wide Dose Requirement
For LLNL to comply with the NESHAPs regulations, the LLNL SW-MEI (defined as the hypothetical member of the public at a single residence, school, business, or office who receives the greatest LLNL-induced EDE from the combination of all radionuclide

source emissions) cannot receive an EDE greater than 10 mrem/y (100 µSv/y). (See Section III for a discussion of the SW-MEI.)

In the spreadsheet, the distance and direction to the respective SW-MEI are shown for each facility at each site. Doses to the site specific SW-MEIs were evaluated for each source and then totaled for site-specific evaluations against the 10 mrem/y dose standard (see Section IV).

0.1 mrem/y Monitoring Requirement
To assess compliance with the requirement for continuous monitoring (potential dose greater than 0.1 mrem/y [1.0 µSv/y] to the maximally exposed public individual or MEI, discussed earlier in Section III), emissions must be individually evaluated from each point source. The location of the MEI is generally different for each emission point. The maximum dose at a location of unrestricted public access typically occurs at a point on the site perimeter. Therefore, it is often referred to as the maximum "fence line" dose, although the off-site maximum dose could occur some distance beyond the perimeter (this could happen, e.g., when the perimeter is close to a stack; however, for nearly all emission points at the Livermore site and Site 300, calculations show that ground level concentrations of radionuclides generally decline continuously beyond LLNL boundaries). As stipulated by the regulations, modeling for assessment of continuous monitoring requirements assumed unabated emissions (i.e., no credit was taken for emission abatement devices, such as filters), but physical state factors and time factors were applied.

The unabated EDE cannot be calculated for HEPA-filtered facilities monitored for radioactive particles. Because the monitoring equipment is placed after HEPA filtration, there is no way to obtain an estimate for what the emissions might have been had there been no filtration. It is not reasonable to apply factors for the effects of the HEPA filters on the emission rate because most of what is measured on the HEPA filters is the result of the radioactive decay of naturally occurring radon, which is capable of penetrating the filter. The spreadsheet gives, for each inventoried point source, the dose to the MEI and the distance and direction to the LLNL fence line where the MEI is located. However, for HEPA-filtered monitored sources, no value is shown.

Source Categories
LLNL radionuclide air emission sources have been classified into seven source categories, indicated by the number in the last column of the following spreadsheet: 1) unmonitored or non-continuously monitored Livermore site facilities that have had a radionuclide usage inventory update for 2007, 2) unmonitored or non-continuously monitored Livermore site facilities with a previous radionuclide usage inventory update, 3) continuously monitored Livermore site and Site 300 facilities, 4) Site 300 explosives experiments, 5) diffuse sources where emissions and subsequent doses were estimated using inventory processes, 6) diffuse sources where emission and dose estimates were supported by environmental surveillance measurements, and 7) sources whose emissions estimates and subsequent doses were estimated by confirmatory air sampling rather than continuous sampling.

Attachment 1 - 2007 LLNL NESHAPs Annual Report Spreadsheet

Building	R m/Ar a	Sta k ID	Op rati n	Radi nu lid s	Annual Inv nt ry with P t ntial f r R l as (Ci)	Physi al Stat Fa t r	Sta k H ight (m)	Sta k Diam t r (m)	Sta k V l ity (m/s)	C ntr l D vi (s)	C ntr l D vi Abat m nt Fa t r	Estimat d Annual Emissi ns (Ci)	Distan t SW-MEI (m)	Dir ti n t SW-MEI	EDE (mr m)	Distan t MEI (m)	Dir ti n t MEI	Unabat d EDE (mr m)	S ur Cat g ry
LIVERMORE SITE POINT SOURCES																			
235	1130	FHE-1A/1B, FHE2A/2B,and FGBE-1A/1B thr ugh FHE-1000/2002	Pr parati n f plut nium sampl s f r diam nd anvil studi s	Gr ss alpha	a	NA	10.7	0.30	6.9	D ubl HEPA	0.0001	0.0E+00	1065	ENE	0.0E+00	b	b	b	3
				Gr ss b ta	a	NA						0.0E+00							
251	1003	FHE-5	G n ral h mistry	Gr ss alpha	a	NA	4.3	0.26	7.6	HEPA	0.01	0.0E+00	1188	E	0.0E+00	b	b	b	3
	1003	FHE-4		Gr ss b ta	a	NA	4.3	0.27	7.6			0.0E+00							
	1142	FHE-8					4.3	0.32	9.9										
	1142	FHE-9					4.3	0.26	3.6										
	1142	FHE-10					4.3	0.28	4.7										
	1150	FGBE-33,34					8.0	0.15	1.8										
	1150	FFE-15					4.3	0.31	6.4										
	1165	FGBE-31,32					5.5	0.87	5.9										
	1211	FHE-6					6.4	0.25	7.0										
	1211	FHE-7					6.4	0.25	8.2										
	1212	FGBE-15,16					5.5	0.10	7.4										
	1232	FGBE-38,39					7.2	0.15	13.4										
	1234	FFE-9					4.3	0.19	2.8										
	1235	FFE-12					4.3	0.25	7.4										
	1235	FGBE-29,30					5.5	0.13	9.3										
	1363	FHE-12					4.3	0.32	10.3										
	1363	FHE-13					5.5	0.28	8.2										
	1364	FFE-23					4.3	0.34	11.9										
	1364	FGBE-35,36					6.4	0.13	9.0										
	1314, 1354	FGBE-44,45					10.2	0.15	3.0										
	H t lls	FGBE-40,41					5.5	0.23	4.7										
	H t lls	FGBE-42,43					5.5	0.36	12.2										
	1150	FFE-13					5.5	0.28	6.0										
251	Gl v B x s	FGBE-1000	Pr vi us transuranic r s ar h	Gr ss alpha	a	NA	7.8	0.30	5.5	Tripl HEPA	0.000001	0.0E+00	1188	E	0.0E+00	b	b	b	3
	Gl v B x s	FGBE-2000		Gr ss b ta			7.8	0.30	6.5										
	R m Exhaust	FFE-1000			a	NA	7.8	0.50	11.9	D ubl HEPA	0.0001	0.0E+00	1188	E	0.0E+00	b	b	b	3
		FFE-2000					7.8	0.50	10.9										
331	All	Sta k 1	Tritium r s ar h and d v l pm nt	H-3	d	1.0E+00	30.0	1.22	6.0	N n	1	5.5E+00	957	ENE	1.3E-03	1384	NE	1.4E-03	3
		Sta k 2	D ntaminati n f parts	H-3	d	1.0E+00	30.0	1.22	7.2	N n	1	9.9E+00							
332	In r m nt 1 R ms	FHE-1000/2000	Plut nium r s ar h	Transuranic s	aa	NA	8.8	0.8x1.1	16.2	D ubl HEPA	0.0001	0.0E+00	912	ENE	0.0E+00	b	b	b	3
332	In r m nt 1 Gl v b x s	FGBE-1000/2000	Plut nium r s ar h	Transuranic s	aa	NA	11	0.3	5.8	Tripl HEPA	0.000001	0.0E+00	912	ENE	0.0E+00	b	b	b	3
332	L ft	FE-4,5W	L ft xhaust	Transuranic s	aa	NA	11	0.6x0.9	4.2	HEPA	0.01	0.0E+00	912	ENE	0.0E+00	b	b	b	3
		FE-4,5E	L ft xhaust	Transuranic s			11	0.6x0.9	3.9	HEPA	0.01	0.0E+00	912	ENE	0.0E+00				
332	In r m nt 1 Gl v b x s	FGBE-3000/4000	Plut nium r s ar h	Transuranic s	aa	NA	11	0.3	6.1	Tripl HEPA	0.000001	0.0E+00	912	ENE	0.0E+00	b	b	b	3
332	In r m nt 1 R m and Gl v b x s	FFE-1000/2000 FGBE-7000/8000	Plut nium r s ar h	Transuranic s	aa	NA	10.1	0.9	11	R m—D ubl HEPA Gl v B x—Tripl HEPA	0.0001 0.000001	0.0E+00 0.0E+00	912	ENE	0.0E+00 0.0E+00	b	b	b	3
							10.1	0.27	2.6										
491	All	FFE-1	St rag	Gr ss alpha	af	NA	9.1	0.9	3.9	D ubl HEPA	0.0001	0.0E+00	1000	SSE	0.0E+00	b	b	b	3
				Gr ss b ta	af	NA						0.0E+00							
695/696	All	DWTF	Wast tr atm nt	Gr ss alpha	d	NA	20.0	1.98	9.9	HEPA Pr -filt r	0.01 0.1	0.0E+00 4.6E-02	953	S	0.0E+00 4.3E-06	198	ENE	3.5E-05	3
				Gr ss b ta	d	NA						0.0E+00							
				Tritium															

Attachment 1 - 2007 LLNL NESHAPs Annual Report Spreadsheet

Building	R mo/Ar a	Sta k ID	Op rati n	Radi nu lid s	Annual Inv nt ry with P t ntial f r R l as (Ci)	Physi al Stat Fa t r	Sta k H ight (m)	Sta k Diam t r (m)	Sta k V l ity (m/s)	C ntr l D vi (s)	C ntr l D vi Abat m nt Fa t r	Estimat d Annual Emissi ns (Ci)	10 mr mr/y Sit -Wid D s R quir m nt Distan t SW-MEI (m)	Dir ti n SW-MEI	EDE (mr m)	0.1 mr mr/y M nit ring R quir m nt Distan t MEI (m)	Dir ti n t MEI	Unabat d EDE (mr m)	S ur Cat g ry
SITE 300 POINT SOURCES																			
Building 801 is th C ntain d Firing Fa ility wh r xpl siv t sts ar ndu t d. This fa ility and th 851 Firing Tabl ar ... indu t d by th D f ns and Nu l ar T hn l gi s Dir t rat																			
801	C ntain d Firing Fa ility	FEFH+1, FE-2	Expl siv t sts	U-238	*	NA	16.8	1.60	4.1	HEPA	0.01	4.9E-08	3770	S	1.1E-07	1809	ENE	1.7E-06	3
				U-235	*	NA				Pr -filt r	0.1	4.2E-10							
				U-234	*	NA						7.7E-09							
Expl siv t sts in whi h radi nu lid s may b pr s nt ar ndu t d n p n-air firing tabl s l at d at Bunk r 851. Th s t sts hav d pl t d uranium mat rial as part f th mat rial inv nt ry. Th r ar multipl t sts p r y ar.																			
851	Firing Tabl		Expl siv t sts	U-238	2.1E-02	1	NA	NA	NA	N n	1	1.0E-03	3170	SSE	3.1E-03	3836	ENE	5.3E-03	4
				U-235	2.7E-04	1						1.3E-05							
				U-234	1.9E-03	1						9.6E-05							
LIVERMORE SITE DIFFUSE SOURCES																			
Building 331 - C ntaminat d quipm nt utsid th fa ility is awaiting transp rt and st rag by Radi a tiv and Hazard us West Manag m nt.																			
331	Outsid		St rag f ntaminat d parts	Tritium	NA	1	NA	NA	NA	N n	1	1.4E+00	957	ENE	4.0E-04	441	SSW	1.4E-03	6
Th Building 612 Yard is p rat d by th Radi a tiv and Hazard us West Manag m nt Divisi n. Th Yard nsists f s v ral ar as wh r ntain rs having radi a tiv wast s ar st r d utd rs. Th ntain rs an utgas tritium.																			
612	Yard		St rag f l w l v l wast	Tritium	NA	1	NA	NA	NA	N n	1	5.5E-01	444	NE	1.0E-03	212	SSW	2.1E-03	6
Th S uth ast Quadrant f th Liv rm r Sit has slightly l vat d l v ls f Pu-239 in th surfa s il and air. Th s ur f th Pu-239 was p st-w st. manag m nt p rati ns.																			
S uth ast Quadrant	Ar a S ur		R susp nsi n	Pu-239	NA	NA	NA	NA	NA	N n	1	NA	NA	NA	4.0E-04	NA	NA	NA	6
SITE 300 DIFFUSE SOURCES																			
Diffus s ur s nsist f r susp nsi n f d pl t d uranium fr m hist ri al xpl siv t sts.																			
Sit 300	A1	Ar a S ur	S il r susp nsi n	U-238	NA	NA	NA	NA	NA	N n	1	NA	NA	NA	3.5E-04	NA	NA	NA	6
				U-235	NA	NA						NA							
				U-234	NA	NA						NA							

NOTE: T nv rt units t b q r ls us 1 Ci=3.7E+10 Bq and t nv rt millir m t si v rts us 1 Sv=1.0E+05 mr m.

*Gr ss alpha and Gr ss b ta missi ns ar ntinu usly m nit r d at th sta k.

B aus m nit ring tak s pla aft r HEPA filtrati n, an unabat d EDE ann t b d t rmin d fr m th m nit ring data (s dis ussi n in S ti n II, subs ti n "R sults f Sta k M nit ring f r Gr ss Alpha and Gr ss B ta Radiati n").

*Sta k missi ns hav b n mbin d as p rmitt d by th EPA/DOE M m random f Und rstanding.

*Tritium HT and HTO missi ns fr m th sta k ar ntinu usly m nit r d.

*Th air m nit ring data f r all missi n p ints sh wn d t tabl r l as f alpha a tivity, l ... th m asur m nts ar at r l w th limit f s nsitivity f th analyti al m th d.

*Air missi ns ar ntinu usly sampl d at th p st-HEPA-filt r atm sph ri dis harg p ints, alth ugh p t ntial missi ns ar l w n ugh that sta k m nit ring is n t r quir d p r th NESHAPs 40 CFR 61 r gulati ns.

*Th unabat d EDE sh wn is nly f r th tritium s ur t rm.

ATTACHMENT 2. ERRATA for the NESHAPs Annual Report

In the *LLNL NESHAPs 2005 Annual Report* (UCRL-TR-113867-06, dated June 2006), one number in Attachment 1 – 2005 LLNL NESHAPs Annual Report Spreadsheet, requires correction, as follows: one page 37 in the EDE column, the dose for Building 251 Unhardened Area should be 0.0E+00 mrem (rather than 6.8E-07 mrem).

In the *LLNL NESHAPs 2006 Annual Report* (UCRL-TR-113867-07, dated June 2007), one number in Table 8 on page 19 requires correction, as follows: the CAP88-PC Dose for the southeast Quadrant (diffuse source) should be 0.00046 mrem/y (rather than 0.00061 mrem/y).